Francis B Nyamnjoh
Stories from Abakwa
Mind Searching
The Disillusioned African
The Convert
Souls Forgotten

Dibussi Tande
No Turning Back. Poems of Freedom
1990-1993

Kangsen Feka Wakai
Fragmented Melodies

Ntemfac Ofege
Namondo. Child of the Water Spirits

Emmanuel Fru Doh
Not Yet Damascus
The Fire Within

Thomas Jing
Tale of an African Woman

Peter Wuteh Vakunta
Grassfields Stories from Cameroon
Majunga Tok: Poems in Pidgin
English
Cry My Beloved Africa
Green Rape: Poetry for the
Environment

Rosemary Ekosso
The House of Falling Women

Peterkins Manyong
God the Politician

Ba'bila Mutia
Coils of Mortal Flesh

Kehbuma Langmia
Titabet and The Takumbeng

Ngessimo Mathe Mutaka
Building Capacity: Using TELL and
African languages as development-
oriented literacy tools

Milton Krieger
Cameroon's Social Democratic Front:
Its History and Prospects as an
Opposition Political party, 1990-
2011

Sammy Oke Akombi
The Raped Amulet
The Woman Who Ate Python &
Other Stories

Susan Nkwentie Nde
Precipice

Francis B Nyamnjoh &
Richard Fonteh Akum
The Cameroon GCE Crisis: A Test
of Anglophone Solidarity

Joyce Ashuntantang &
Dibussi Tande
Their Champagne Party Will End!
Poems in Honor of Bate Besong

John Percival
The 1961 Cameroon Plebiscite:
Choice or Betrayal

Albert Azeyeh
Reussite Scolaire, Faillite Sociale:
Généalogie mentale de la crise de
l'Afrique Noire Francophone

T0198534

1

Beware The Drives

Sammy Oke Akombi

Langaa Research & Publishing CIG
Mankon, Bamenda
Publisher:
Langaa RPCIG
(*Langaa* Research & Publishing Common Initiative Group)
P.O. Box 902 Mankon
Bamenda
North West Province
Cameroon
Langaagrp@gmail.com
www.langaapublisher.com

Distributed outside N. America by African Books Collective

orders@africanbookscollective.com

www.africanbookscollective.com

Distributed in N. America by Michigan State University Press

msupress@msu.edu

www.msupress.msu.edu

ISBN:9956-558-85-0

© Sammy Oke Akombi 2008
First Published 2008

DISCLAIMER
All views expressed in this publication are those of the author and do not necessarily reflect the views of Langaa RPCIG.

To my little Boy, Epi who's been an
invaluable source of inspiration

Contents

Introduction

This collection of verse, which has mostly short poems, some of which are two-liners, is an outcome of several years of keen observation of the very nature of man. The observation brought this writer to the conclusion that man is dominated by fear and in his effort to conquer it, he resorts to unbridled aggression. Such aggression has been very instrumental in much of the success that humanity has been able to achieve, so far. But at the same time, the same aggression in man's nature has been responsible for the pleasure he takes in the ruthless destruction of his own kind, the environment in which he cushions himself, plants and animals.

There's therefore no denying that the aggressive instincts in man play both positive and negative roles and it can't be helped but accepted as an essence of human existence. For humans to take advantage of it, they should master its positive role by putting it under control. This is where this collection comes handy. It provides an awareness of such aggressive instincts and appeals to man to:

> *Check their steps*
> *In the dance*
> *Towards the unknown.*
> (from *A Fervent Wish*)

Many of the poems in the collection provide this awareness and some go further to suggest what man should do, like in:

> *Regals*
> *Regals always relieve the weight of life*
> *Off the shoulders of the living.*
> *The living like a traveler on foot*
> *Must from time to time put down their load*
> *To pause and ponder for a rest.*

As a social observer and poet, I wish to opine that among other virtues, love and peace stand out strongly to put human aggression under control. Here's what the poet says about love:

> *A Wand*
> *Love is neither wealth nor poverty*
> *It is neither ugliness nor beauty*
> *Nor is it personality, responsibility*
> *Accountability, integrity and ability!*
> *Love is simply love:*
> *A magic wand that turns on the light.*
> *It is through love that we can see clearly where we are*
> *coming from and where we are going. …it's a treasure, /*
> *'cause it's so true and pure / That it's unbelieving.*
>
> (from *It Takes a Lifetime*)

The role of love in attenuating human aggression is typified in the following lines:

> *Love in all its sacredness enhances*
> *The same engenders headaches*
> *That disenchant.*
> *But we must!*
> *We must love, all the same*
> *To keep fear in check.*
> (from the poem *Beware the Drives*)

When we love, we shall definitely *keep fear in check*. We shall be spared several embarrassments like the ones expressed in poems like *Insecurity, Tell Me, What Makes Them Tick?* And in *Brother Suicide Bomber* whom if he had had any sense of love, would not *impose on innocent others / the same dismal fate* he had imposed on himself.

On the role of peace as a soothing factor on human aggression, we can identify this in *A Dove* where a clarion call is made to the whole of humanity to imbibe the sterling qualities of a dove. Other poems for peace include*: Peace, The Flag of Peace, Give a Piece, Finding Peace, No Need to Lose Blood.*

In this writer's search for a possible solution to the human aggression problem, he also explores the intricacies of child development in poems like: *Victims, No Greater Awe, Quite Depressing*. The poet provokes an awareness that children brought up in a society of bad habits would invariably grow up to be bad. Therefore world communities, (through *The Family ...The only grouping / coupled with cords of calibre)*, are called upon to be careful in the way their children are brought up. Better nurtured children engender a better nurtured world.

All the one hundred and twenty-seven poems, in spite of their diverse themes *(poverty, corruption, self-confidence, materialism, etc)*, shoot arrows at the possible control of human aggression, so that a better world can emerge. One of the poems at the close of the collection, *Ahmadou's Deathbed*, which incidentally is the longest, x-rays the life of a former leader of a people, whose aggressive instincts had taken him too far. He only realizes the excesses of his exploits only on his dying bed, far away from the country he had been aggressive for. In the company of only one out of his millions of compatriots, he recounts his deeds and misdeeds. He is very remorseful but unfortunately he had no opportunity to make amends. He could *hear death knocking with so much urgency*. His story however drives in a loud message to existing leaders: beware the drives that drive you on.

The entire humanity is invariably called upon, through this collection to **Beware the Drives** as we all seek a way forward, for ourselves and our world. In this regard, the poet starts the collection with his own epitaph in which he makes a strong appeal to humanity:

> *You too, poet or no poet, sure shall find peace*
> *In doing pieces, for yourself and mankind.*

A Poet's Epitaph

Here lies one who had the privilege
To stay alive for quite a while.
While alive he roamed the wilds
And then found peace
In doing pieces, for himself and mankind.
You too, poet or no poet, sure shall find peace
In doing, pieces, for yourself and mankind.

Tell Me

Tell me!
I say, tell me.
Why did you do it?
Don't look at me like that
As if you know not, what I'm talking about.

Tell me! Why did you do it?
You told a lie, a malicious lie
Which has made someone die
See, what lies there
A body stoned to death
Because you did it, you lied.
You! Your warped mind
Full of intrigue, envy, caprice, malice and avarice

Look at the result. What insult.
Hopes shattered and splattered
Waiting to be buried
All because of you, your warped mind
With so much evil entrenched.
Full of intrigue, envy, caprice, malice and avarice
Do you and your likes, do spar the world bits
and bits of peace.

Hurdles

When the gods watch a race
They watch out for its pace.
They sit down for some races
And for some, they're bound to sit up.
How their bliss blows up
When they must sit up.
So, there's no race
The gods look forward to
Like a race with hurdles.
The swifter the hurdles
The sweeter the victories,
Which even they, the gods
Cheer the victor up.

Beware the Drives

Beware the drives. They take you to the top.
The same drives, drive you down the bottom.
Love in all its sacredness enhances
The same engenders headaches
That disenchant.
But we must!
We must love, all the same
To keep fear in check.

Victims

When children, innocent and clean
As they always have been
Die in storms and quakes –
Earthquakes, techno-quakes, hunger-quakes
Socio-politico-ideologico-quakes
And then gun and bomb quakes,
One can't help but question,
Is that why they were born?

My Mind

Sometimes the mind, my mind boils
Over the naked fact that
Rapists, rogues and rascals
Infesting streets and alleyways
Making them dangerous
Were once helpless babies.

No Greater Awe

There's no greater awe
Than that a squalling toddler
Shoots up to be:
A Jesus Christ
A Mohammed
        Or
An Abraham Lincoln
A Nelson Mandela
        Or
An Adolf Hitler
A Bagdad butcher.

There's no greater awe.

Quite Depressing

Quite depressing
When a kid points
At another kid, born of his father
And says: *there goes my enemy for life.'*
Even more so
When people of the world
Children of one God
Get so scared, about their enemies for life.

Won't Mother Stop?

I thought she would stop
But she hasn't stopped.
She hasn't stopped
Crying every other day.

She had thought they would stop
But they haven't stopped.
They haven't stopped
Dying, every other day.

No Curse

Poverty, isn't as bad as a curse.
It changes its course
When the will has recourse
To its willing resource.

No Scare

Poverty shouldn't scare
It should make you stare
Then think and glow.

Fortune's Path

The twist of destiny's sometimes whimsical
It makes you grow skeptical
Then swings around to be musical
Which is only logical
For fortune's path's hardly ornamental.

Art

Perfection in art seems all nonsense
As there's always some sense
In what the artist has left undone.

Justice

The first time the police came
Searching
I asked them for a search warrant.
They beat me up silly and I thought
They were marauders, not the police.
I sought justice but never found it.
The next time they came,
My eyes met my scars
And I let them do as they pleased.

Courage

If helpless babies
Can bear the blows of existence
Why should adults surrender to suicide
In their inability to bear same.

The Harvest

It's in times of crisis that the harvest
Of men is most fruitful.
It's in times like that, that men
Are easily picked out among women.

Reluctant Democracy

In a reluctant democracy
Lies are only lies
When they score no goal.
When they score a goal,
They justify the actions of the liar
Or those of his master.

Enjoying A Symphony

When a man, enjoying a symphony, in the safety of his
balcony
Throws invectives and missiles at a despondent crowd
I wonder how he feels
If somehow, he becomes part of the cacophony.

Leadership

Leadership in a spurious democracy
Has got such a strong viscous
Leaving it means tearing away.

What Makes Them Tick

What makes a leader tick
Isn't how much they deceive
But how much they conceive.

Courts Must Count

When the courts cease to count
Where else
Justice can be sought on earth.

Appreciation

The goodness of writing
Is in the goodness of knowing
That someone out there
In the maddening crowd
Can step aside
And give your work a nod.

Thank God For Chissano

Joachim in his quiet corner
Did his best for Mozambique
To fetch deserved peace for her
In spite of the hurdles on his path
He did what he could and left the rest
To fellow man and to God.

Civil Slavery

If slavery is the provision of bread
To the slave
Enough to make him live
And not die
So he can be exploited
Until his bones sigh,
Then our civil service is a huge slave camp.

Life

When people delight in destroying life
They simply forget they need life
In order to enjoy life.

Living

What really counts in living
Is making people feel like living.

Soldiers of Life

Life's like a raging war
Soldiers fight and fall
But the war rages on.

Regals

Regals always relieve the weight of life
Off the shoulders of the living.
The living like a traveller on foot
Must from time to time put down their load
To pause and ponder for some rest.

Bliss and Adversity

In bliss
Minds shift to the abundance of life
In adversity
They drift to the wastefulness of life.

Modesty and Vanity

Modesty can cope
With both prosperity and adversity.
But vanity can cope
Only with prosperity.

Freedom

Decrees and laws
Can ban all freedoms
But freedom of thought,
Which floors all flawns.

Intolerance

With forty-two Presidents
Down in the history books
Americans are proud, very proud to
Put them side by side.
We've got just two
And it's hard, so hard to
Put them side by side.

Failure

Failure in search of nobility
Finds success in acceptability
And also in humility.

Uncle Sam

Sitting and watching
A Bush smile
While
A Clinton undresses him
Of all his garments of pomp
And power,
I just wished
In spite of myself
I were a part of that cabin.

Identity

At Norfolk, some folks
Spat at me
Because I'm African.

In Cairo, some folks
Spat at me
Because I'm Cameroonian.

In Cape Town, some folks
Spat at me
Because I'm not South African.

In Yaounde, Some folks
Spat at me
Because I'm silly *Anglo*.
Where then and when
Will folks stop
Spitting at me?

Experience

My experiences depend
On my troubles
The more troubles I've got
The more experienced
I become.

Mistakes

An advantage with mistakes
Is that they plunge us
Into gruesome experiences
Which if we come out successful
They stay for a long time useful.

Conscience

Count not on conscience
At all times
It loses patience
And goes to sleep
When evil gets the grip.

Cause and Effect

The cause is drinking
The illness, drunkenness.

Destiny

The slower you go
The slower you get there.
The faster you go
The faster you get there.

Priority

Everyone
Their priority
And priority depends on
The ability
To acquire what you require.

Love and Truth

When love and truth
Intertwine
Then perfection is at hand.

Women

Women go down as beings of great tolerance.
They can cope with
Both the ugliness
Of the heart and that of the face.

Wives

Wives shouldn't be appalled
When husbands resort to beating
They do it for want of giving something.
 If they can't get what they wish to give.
They simply give what they can give.

Expectations

In life, no one
Ever meets the expectations
Of anyone
Even the creator
Never meets the expectations
Of his creations

Bitterness

Often we dissect a man in our bitterness
And to public expose his bad ways.
But remember, he's got trickles of goodness
Which cannot be counted as useless.

Agents of Evil

In honest living, agents of evil
Are forever present to cause ill will.
Never yield to their intentions
Which always are mere distractions.

Sycophants

Sycophants are smart at knowing the powerful
But they hardly know the difference
Between civil and evil.

Criticism

When persons are criticized
To be corrected
Then criticism is meant for the living
And not for the dead.

Twisted Minds

Twisted minds hardly go further
Than the tiny cells yonder.

Vice and Virtue

Virtue compensates for lack of beauty.
And
Vice is for some time
Virtue for all the time.

Cameroon

Lying in calm, in the arms
Of her curious neighbours.
Her trimmed head falling back
On the cushious of the fresh waters of lake Chad.
And then feet astride; the right
Stretching out to the brawling waters
of the Atlantic.
And the left
To the exuberant heart
of the equatorial rain forest.

A Reminder

When Hutus and Tutsis
Were *hutuing* and *tutsying* one another
They had simply forgotten
They were brothers and sisters
Whose destiny depended on
The construction of a single roof: Rwanda.

My Commitment

In humility, I commit Myself to Cameroon, My country
Land of peace, promise and serenity.
To be loyal and alert to her unity,
Promote the peace and uphold the promise.
To the Almighty, I entrust, this commitment.

Poetry

Poetry like all creation
Hardly is satisfactory in the perception of the creator.
There always is something that should have been done.
But it is always a mystery in the perception of the
spectator.
Always there's something to be understood
That hasn't been understood

Two Fighting

Finally
When you ask them
Why they're fighting,
They can't even find the breath
To explain.

Peace

Peace is the closest of things
To the heart of human beings
Yet it's so hard
To look for it around
And find.

The Flag of Peace

Keep the flag, the flag of peace flying
For it'll curb much, too much suffering
And spare the world so much crying
Which is caused by too much dying.

A Dove

A dove in its every act exudes, love and peace.
O let this be for a man in their every act.

Give a Piece

You can make so much peace
Just by giving a piece
Of what you've got.

Finding Peace

Happiness, pure and true
Is in finding peace
In your finds
And then enjoy them, pure and true.

No Need To Lose Blood

A bite of the Bight of Biafra
Once provoked a terrible war
In which many were gone
Who weren't supposed to go.
And many haven't been born
Who were supposed to be born.
What a waste!

And then the longing for a bite of Bakassi.
Still in the Bight of Biafra.
Two big brothers stood face to face
Wrangling over whose bite it was.
They flexed their muscles, their lances off their sheaths
Shone dazzlingly in the scorching sun
And the pores on both brothers poured out sweat.
Both were visibly lust for blood.
Then a dove with an olive branch in its beak
Flew quietly on the scene.
As soon as it was seen
The brothers realized, there was no need to lose blood.

Brother Suicide Bomber

Brother suicide bomber
Your inability to withstand the pressures
Of the raging battle
Have made you decide to quit.
Why impose on innocent others
The same dismal fate.

Nothing Counts

Nothing counts so much as
When in the course of your work
You make others pick up a smile.
And walk a mile
Without pausing awhile.

Worth

Worth!
It grows
Only when it is acknowledged.

In A Boeing

Sitting strapped and looking down
The entire world at my feet.
I feel I'm at no one's but God's own feet.
He had created the sun, seas, land and animals
And saw that it was good.
Then the moon, stars, man and woman
And saw that it was good.
Man then created planes, cities and farms
Me thinks, He saw that it was good.

Paris-Chicago

When I fly, fly far above
I think of the dove.
Wishing all on board price peace
As much as it does.

Hard Times

When the times go insane...
All people, the rich and the poor alike
Deserve a pat on the back
For managing to live at all.

The Youth

Jobs are rare and the times are hard
These times.
Yet I see them scuttling
To and fro their schools
Everyday
Twice a day.
Hence I know all isn't lost yet.
There's still vitality in the youth.

Importance of The Whole

Taking care of ourselves
Isn't so much for the selves
As for the whole
The selves soon fade away
But the whole would forever stay.

The Whole Story

Life's but a tangled dream
Long drawn for some
For some, just plain brief.
One gets up from it only
In death – the reality of life.

Language

Language is like money.
Stop using it,
And you lose all
That's honey.

Your Pleasure And Your Treasure

Acquiring a language is as much a pleasure
As it is a treasure
Acquiring two makes you bilingual
So bilingualism doubles both:
Your pleasure and your treasure.

It Doesn't Make Sense

It doesn't make sense
When you shout at and jackboot
Fellow man
For one odd day, another man
Will shout at you and boot your arse.

It doesn't make sense
When you eat alone
While others gape and yawn in hunger
For when it comes to a fight
You'd fight your fight alone.

It doesn't make sense
When you give priority
To money, over people.
'Cause on the day you swoon
And up points your nose,
People, not money shall grieve your loss.

It doesn't make sense
When you think
You're demi-god.
For when you crash, crumble and die
The world lives and kicks high and high.

It Takes A Lifetime

It takes a lifetime to find love
And even then, many are they
Who spend a lifetime without finding it.
When found, it's a treasure
'Cause it's so true, innocent and pure
That it's unbelieving

It burns eternal, never relenting
Like the flames of the sun.
Some great, great finds
Have been known to be inaccessible
But you'll only need to be sensible
To enjoy the fruits of love, so true
Innocent and pure that it's unbelieving.

A Magic Hand

Love is neither wealth nor poverty
It is neither ugliness nor beauty
Nor is it personality, responsibility
Accountability, integrity and ability!
Love is simply love:
A magic wand that turns on the light.

Recovery

If the living ever recovered
From death
As they do from ill-health
Then, the business
Of living would be better scored.

A Rebirth

Recovery from illness is like a rebirth
Life's faced with greater vitality and humility
As the spirits enjoy the balm of reality
Which is positive to morality.

I Wonder

I wonder, this superiority
of humanity over animality
Animals take no booze nor cocaine.
Make no toxics nor guns nor bombs
Cheat no one nor rob nor murder.
Practise no partiality, nor tribalism, nor terrorism.

Think of no wars and destruction
Neither do they of abduction and abortion.
Nor do they of deception and corruption,
Make love just for procreation
And never, never, never for recreation.

So, I wonder, this superiority
Of humanity over animality.

Whither The Claims

Whither the claims of humanity
When humans've lost their sense of dignity
And treat humans unlike humans:
Rile humans
Rob humans
Rape humans
Rip humans
Whither the claims of humanity.

It's known, humans've got the blessings
Of brains besides brawn and instincts
Why the absence of the sense of dignity
And integrity.
Thus they treat their likes unlike humans.
Cheating their likes
Battering their likes
Crushing their likes
Hanging their likes
Whither the claims of humanity.

Beasts they say've got no blessings of brains
But they're more humane than humans.
Never seek the cushions of heroin
Nor those of a fag
Nor cannabis
Nor booze
Nor guns and bombs.
Whither the claims. The claims of humanity.

The Prairie Lights

The Prairie Lights have shown the light
That books and poetry are
The admirals and field marshals
Of the raging battle for life.

The Iowa Riverside

Soft ripples gently sweep
Through the surface of the river.
Ducks and swans happily swim up
Stream, mid-stream and down-stream
Across and about in gratitude to the giver.
The quietude is a servitude for creation
A perfect place for a writer.

No Need For A Queue

It flows with so much ease
As if to beckon peace: please
Come, please peace come.
Elsewhere the world's in a coma
Come here for the rescue
There's no need for a queue.

Avoid The Back

Avoid the back as you do the plague
For of course not much good comes off it
Backache
Backward
Backwoods
Backwaters
Backfire
Backbite
Backstab
Avoid the back to avoid the aches.

Pride

We've got the pride, pride of a self
We don't mind tearing one another a piece
For the sake of keeping this pride, pride of the self

We've got the pride, pride of a family
We don't mind tearing one another a piece
For the sake of keeping this pride, pride of the family.

We've got the pride, pride of a nation
We don't mind tearing one another a piece
For the sake of keeping the pride, pride of the nation

We've got the pride, pride of a religion
We don't mind tearing one another a piece
For the sake of keeping the pride, pride of the religion.

We should try the pride, pride of a world
Where all folks are only folks and what reigns' peace
For the sake of keeping the pride, pride of the world.

My Mother

Were I to choose before I was born
Never would I have been
My mother's baby
Destitute woman, sick of poverty.

But then: she's all I've got for an umbrella
            she's all I've got for a mother
            I can only accept, admire and love her
            and all that she's wont to offer.
When I'm in dire need
of drying off balls, of tears off my cheeks
I crawl to her, and not to
The other woman, clad in gold.

Insecurity

Insecurity has become
Mortals's chief currency.
When they bypass one another
The hi and hellos are
As if to say:
Please don't hurt me.

The Biggest Upset

The biggest upset as I grow older
Is the realization that sooner
Or later, I'd grow bald
Bald of my contemporaries:
The good and bad people
Who make living matter to me.

Tears

The tears that wet your pillow
Every other night
Can't spare me the thought:
Why, why do bad things happen
To good people?
Answer: only good people
Have the strength of mind
To overcome bad things.

Misfortune

Fall not to pieces
When misfortune comes your way.
Because the sadness of the day
Surely ushers in
The happiness of another day.

Solutions

The solutions we contrive
In the face of difficulty
Are bequeathed to humanity.
So seek solutions
No matter the difficulty

The Madona In My Dream

Neither you nor I, knew not
As the gods kept playing on a knot
Though doubts and fears may dare enter
Towering hope always stands to conquer
You it is that was, the Madonna in my dream.

Globilisation

To me it's yet unknown
Where to place my napkin at meal
Which hand for the fork,
Which for the knife and which for the spoon,
And here comes the chopstick.

Fall Out

On a fine Tuesday evening
I was watching
A sports programme on tee-vee
Suddenly it dawned on me
I knew by name all the players
Of Olympique Marseille
But knew none of those playing
For Olympique Mvolye.
Who says we're done with colonialism.

Colonised Mind

I write as I think.
Too bad, my thoughts
Come down in the tongue I was taught
At school.
Not in the tongue of my birth.

Once I Begged Some Fish

Once I begged some fish from a fisherman
He gave me some, which I took home
And made my family feel at home.

The next time he saw me , he read in my eyes
The supplicating looks, worn only by beggars.
In his boat he took me, and taught me, how to fish.

He taught me good, how to fish
And I've known well how to fish
But still, I can't make my family feel at home
Because I fish in very troubled waters.

Development

Development is not:
Riding high in a big luxury car
Living big in a big house
And sitting big on big chair.
While a vast majority stares
Wondering if dinner'll be there.

Development is not:
The eternal outpouring
Of filthy smoke
From the flue of factory chimneys
Nor the dumping of toxic wastes
In rivers, seas and the bowels of mother earth.

It is not
The multiplication of lethal arsenal
Nor the passionate nurturing
Of fierce dogs of war.
Nor is it the acquisition of tricks diabolical
To pull a trigger on humanity.

Development is:
The meticulous nurturing of human minds
To respect God and the worth of humanity
Be relentless in the safeguard of mother earth
And walk upright to work, for the sake of dignity.

Chain Smoker

Glowing sticks, stick on his lips
Like flaring gas on an escape pipe.
His nostrils pipe out sickening smoke
Like the flue
Of a factory chimney.

To John Keats and His Likes

So brief it was your life
But it held brief
For those in grief.
Your courage in adversity
Still soothes souls in diversity
The words that make your art
Guide humans as they act.

Misdeeds

A bank's been robbed
And business' gone cold
How cruel

A house's been burgled
And the tenants' left in a pool of blood
What cruelty!

A woman's been raped
In the full glare of her man.
O, how cruel!

A child has been kidnapped
And a ransom has been asked for
It's so cruel.

An entire nation's been raped
And left reeking in pain.
O, what cruelty!

What cruelty!
It's hard, so hard to believe
That the perpetrators of the deeds
Were once innocent babies
Fragile and vulnerable.

Shall We Ever Get There?

The world in my nature:
One that everyone loves nature
And hates indeed to capture
And place under torture
Animals and plants they should nurture
And assure all and sundry a picture
Of a green and not a grim future.

Shall we ever get there?
The world in my nature.

Brains Like Grains

As farmers cultivate grain
So do teachers cultivate brain.
The success of each depend
On the success of their yield.
And even so, the yield depends
On the richness of the field.
Indeed, brains like grains
Depend on the richness of the field.

A Fervent Wish

How I wish
The world were tranquil
It'll make humans
Hear the heartbeat of others
And the bidding of God.

How I wish
Every folk were kind and gentle.
It'll make humans
Feel concerned about the mess
That's spilling out.

How I wish
Time, for a second, stood still.
It'll make man and woman
Check their steps
In the dance
Towards the unknown.

Dear Oppressor

Suppress a man
And he might succumb, crumble
And then die.

Suppress the truth
And it'll succumb but not crumble.
It'll never die.

Suppress it further
And it'll grumble, rumble
And then ignite and burn
Growing into a mighty inferno.

Poor Us

Over the decades
We've been so used to being
So undemocratic
That
Our own process of being
Quite democratic
Is such a ridiculous rigmarole.

Fooling You

If for respect sake, you
Don't let those who fool you
Know, you know they're fooling you
Then, they'll think fooling you
Is the best, they can do for you.

An Enemy

Oftentimes, an enemy
Of the state
Is a darling
Of the people.
In a state like that
I'm at pains whom
To state
As the real enemy.

Most of The Time

Most of the time
Fighters of freedom
Fight as much not for themselves
As for others.

Seers

Those who see with their minds
May have no need for their eyes
For they see better than those
Who see only with their eyes.

Importance of Past

Considering the past spills into the present
And the present into the future
Then the underpinning of life is the past,
Which no wise should waive.

The Family

Of groups, small or big
The only grouping
Coupled with cords of calibre
Is the family.

Living in, and as a family,
Conquering stands to conquer.
So at home live in a family.
And at work, as a family.

Inextricable Knot

Family! The microcosm of a nation.
It's got its geniuses. It's got its fools.
It's got its virtuous. It's got its vicious.
It's got its fickle. It's got its faithful.
But it's a knot that stays knotted
Like that of a tie on the neck of banker at work.

Materialism

Where everywhere what counts
Is materialism
Intellectuals hawk intellectualism
With talented impunity.

Thoughts on Corruption

I
Corruption
Is the meanest of options
For lovers of peace and justice.

II
The need of a nation
What the nation needs
Is devotion
Not corruption

III
Poverty in material
Isn't as genial
To corruption
As is poverty in spirit.

IV
Creativity stops
Where corruption begins.

V
The most unusual friend
Of fairness
Is none other than corruption.

VI
Corruption is a housefly
On an open sore,
Which is conscience.

VII
A healthy conscience
Is the best judge
Of cases of corruption.
The guilty are sentenced
To varying terms of fake life.

VIII
It's an exercise in futility
To build up perennial wealth
On corruption.

IX
Corruption is like sinking sand
On which no solid foundation can stand.

X
Kick out corruption
And the vacuum
Will be replaced by invention.

XI
A corrupt mind
Is a disturbed mind

XII
There's always a boomerang
When corruption slips into the rank.

XIII
The grand creator created creatures
To create and not corrupt
In order for them to complete
The creation process
Which must culminate
In a grand redemption.

XIV
Corruption drowns
Corruption drowns:
Success
And progress
Ambition
And direction

Affection
And reflection
Democracy
And meritocracy
In a deep pool of freedom.

XV
A little bit of corruption
Belittles nobility.

XVI
If a sound sleep means
Anything to anyone
Let the one shun
To be corrupt and be corrupted.

XVII
If you mind corruption
All you need to fight it, is your mind.

XVIII
The day
everyone in their every corner
Decides to turn their back
Against corruption
There would be no greater heaven
On earth.

Give Them A Chance

We get so cross and snap and scold
Those whom we lord over
For those faults that may spill over
Because of no fault of theirs.

We simply adore the habit of finding
Faults, cursing and reprimanding
The feeble folk, from whom we expect too much
Far too much,
Measuring them by the yardstick of so much.

Yet they've got so much that's good, fine and pure.
So much that gets one out of a feeling of blue.
But we ignore, because we're plagued by the plague:
Impatience.
Be true then and make a turn around, for atonements.

Never Think They're A Fool

Never think they're a fool
The one who never does as you do.
You may take a short time
To do what you want to do
And they may take twice the time.
But still does what you want to do.

Never think they're a fool
The one who never does as you do.
You may have the nerve to do
What you want to do
While they may have no nerve but verve
To do what you want to do.

Always think there's a difference
Between you and the others
The things they do relate to their need
And their need depends on their greed.
The things you do may depend on your creed
Which you can see, may not be theirs.

Kill No Man For God's Sake

The grandeur of God is such that
His ways are so grandiose.
God sees the ways of man
Like man sees the ways of ants.
Ants that man tramples upon
At his pace and at his ease.
Even when in a single file, they're lined up.
Be it for a binge or for a dirge.

The pettiness of man is such that
He makes himself a soldier of God
And goes to war, though his God
Carries a great flame of peace.
A flame that licks up
Any goading, insult and derision.
For God's sake!
Man! Know yourself
And kill no man, for God's sake.

How Honest Are You?

Tell me! You, tell me!
How honest are you?
In using your ability
with so much agility
to nudge and urge,
a man, who's spent over half a century,
listening to the same things
saying the same things
reading the same things
and writing the same things,
in the same place,
to stay on and on, to do these same things
in the same place.
Tell me …eh! Tell me!
How honest are you?

My Little Boy

And my little boy wrote:
What the hell are you doing out there?
Daddy come back quick.
I'm glad to tell you, my headache's gone.
My stomachache too and earache are gone.
You daddy, shouldn't be gone.
Come back to me, come back quick.

My little boy, who else but you
Can write words like these.
Words of one who cares.
I know you care, you care so much
And back I'll come. Come back to you.
Though it'll not be so soon.

Everyday, every hour, every minute
The words come back to me and I read them
Even as they pierce my heart.
They make me feel your warmth and I wonder:
What would I have been
If you hadn't been.

Resilience

In spite of all
Embedded in human nature
Is resilience
An admirable feature.
In one moment, man's sweating, swearing and cursing.
Yet in another,
He's all promise, hope and merry-making.

Value Scale Balance

In the business of life
The value of a man
Hangs on the man.
A thief must know he's a thief
And knows how much weight he carries.
A fraud knows he's a fraud
And knows how much weight he carries
And takes it to the value scale balance.

Happiness

Happiness isn't in the set goal.
For once attained it shifts to another goal.
And as long as you live,
There always will be goals.
Therefore happiness is for now
In everything you do now.
When it is growing up
Grow up happily.
When it is making others grow,
Do it happily.
When it is a project to carry out,
Do it happily.
If it is nursing a spouse,
Nurse them happily.
If it is trekking to work
Trek on merrily
If it is riding to work
Ride on merrily.
If it is driving an 'oldsmobile'
Drive on joyfully.
Happiness is there, in everything you do now.

Find It

There's happiness in those old shoes of yours.
Find it.
There's happiness in that humble home of yours.
Find it.
There's happiness in that boring job of yours.
Find it.
There's happiness in that ugly man of yours.
Find it.
There's happiness in that lame child of yours.
Find it.
There's happiness in that poor country of yours.
Find it.
There's happiness even in an ailing life. Find it!

Being Upright

Of my many hobbies, the one I adore sorely
Is watching a crowded world roll by
Such a rattling rat race.
Hordes of women and men, craving for happiness.
I'd craved for it myself and searched for it everywhere.
Recently, only recently I realised, it was in uprightness.
Only in uprightness.
When you're upright, everything's all right.
And when all's right, there's nothing to tear.
And when there's nothing to tear, there's no fear.
And when there's no fear, happiness' boundless.
Therefore, there's everything in a being, being upright.

Two Wills

On the shores of Lake Michigan
I saw well-mannered nature
In the unobtrusive expanse of water.
So dignifying, in a bid to nurture
Birds flying skywards, and humanity.
So peaceful, so wonderful, so sure
As the waves gently washed themselves ashore.
Ah what sublimity.

When I turned about and backed the lake
It was hotels, offices and cathedrals, flying skywards.
Rail lines snaking through the city and disappearing
downwards.
Overhead bridges meandering and crisscrossing the
streets
Peppering the scurrying changes.
Such un-dignifying arrogance, in a bid to beat nature.
It's turbulent, terrible and unsure
As herds of humans still trod along to nobody knew
where.
Ah what calamity.

When I stepped off the spot, I saw that
The difference was clear.
The difference between two wills.
The will of God and the will of man.

At Ahmadou's Deathbed

Ahmadou's deathbed was at a tight corner in a dismal
room
Even though he's got great palaces with several rooms.
After watching him cough, curse, cough and curse,
cough, curse…
I coughed in turn, and then told him whom I was.
Opened-eyed, he said weakly: o compatriot, I've had so
few around.
I've had so few come to me ever since I ceased being
grand comrade.
I'm glad, so glad, you're here to watch me die.
I've for long looked forward to something more than a
germane sigh.
Ah the good past, compared to this woeful present.

I saw his feeble face light up and his imagination went
ablast.
I A-aaa-a-ahmadou, an unknown northern star,
Shot down south, seeking what fate
For me, may have in store.
I ran into the luck of being picked up as a courier,
Exposing me to all kinds of things, people and cultures.
I met and made both friend and foe.
I keenly watched the ranting and wrangling of both ants
and bulls,
Nationalists they said they were.
It made some sense, lots of sense and I got keen.
The friends I made propped me high.
And shortly I was one of those to reckon with.
I tangoed with Prime Ministers and became one myself.
I couldn't believe my fortune,
Which kept propelling me in spite of my humble self.
I became a great architect – an architect of a nation.
A nation of a people who had been fragmented.
Fragmented by the might of colonization.

It couldn't have been easy. It needed toughness and so I
got tough.
I maimed where I had to maim.
I burnt down where I had to burn
And I murdered where I had to murder.

To keep a seat, so hot, so much dirt had to accumulate.
The people, whose leader I was grew more and more
feeble and I liked it.
They called me their Draco and I liked that.
The fear I had sowed in their hearts, had made them toe
the lines I forged.
The lines I knew were good for progress.
The lines I knew were good for success.
The north, whose star I was,
Needed to catch up with the south.
Those who had been fooled by English,
I made sure they were *unfooled* by French.
A little over a decade, my knitting was done.
It wasn't easy but it had to be.
Very high-handed I was, to enforce high-mindedness.
I brought honour, pride, pomp and pageantry.
I kept things going for another decade,
Ensuring oneness, uprightness and brotherhood.
They adored me, they worshipped me, my people.
A convoqued compatriot, would pee in his trousers,
Because of the uncertainties of my convocations.
And yet there were many, who were convoqued for
reward.
Steadily my might heightened.
And I thought I could do like the Almighty: simply do
and undo.

So, one fine day, I took the entire nation by storm.
I told them, I'd done enough for them
And I'd groomed an heir, to take up the baton.
An heir from the south, where my luck had emerged.
Trust him, as you trusted me.

He sure shall follow my footsteps and our nation shall continue to surge.
Surge forward to greatness.

But see me now compatriot, I'm unable to undo what I'd done.
Quietly I'm dying on an alien bed in an alien land.
The guards in their thousands that I used to have,
Not even one stands by my deathbed.
Were it not for you, I wouldn't have had the pleasure to confide in a compatriot
As I make my exit. I can hear death knocking with so much urgency.
In case it picks me up, while you're still here, tell them, tell them back home.
Tell them, all the compatriots, the young and the old that I do acknowledge my faults.
They were quite grave and even very grave, but I was doing all for the common good.
For the sustainability of a young nation.
Now that I die in this dismal room, I've learnt, many a lesson.
Lots more than the ones learnt, all the decades spent, lording it over them – my people.
I know even my mortal remains may never commune with the land of its birth.
However, I die not minding the humiliation – I've learnt to know that life's only ...
Oh – o – o this cough ... cough ...cough ...
co...co...fffff......

The Tinker

Amazing, how the tinker tinkers boxes!
He does it so well, they always sway his way.
He's so good at: tinkering institutions
that he tinkers them to equally sway his way,
and tinkering calculations
that he tinkers them to swell his way,
and also the population
that he tinkers it to swell his way.
He even tinkers the formulations
which commingle the people, their ways and their
nation.
He does it so well, they sway his way.
Where his tinkering falters and falls flat is in:
the desperate tinkering of the thinker.
The tinker has in vain tinkered the thinker.
Vain, because the thinker is uprightness and truth.
I swear, in the ongoing dispensation,
give way to thinkers, not tinkers.

Writer On The Run

Ink like water
Quenches the thirst of a writer.
Once it starts flowing down, on paper
Ideas follow, flowing on its trail
Like locomotive wheels on rail.

For Everything, Thank God
Thank God for the people.
All the people I wine and dine with.
Thank God for the safety of the people.
All the people I have no cause to wine and dine with.
Thanks for the strength
That's enabled me to commune with mother earth.
Thank God for all mercies, and being so forgiving.
Thanks and thanks mightily, for love and everything.